W9-CDC-714

A Guide for Using

Sarah, Plain and Tall

and

Journey

in the Classroom

Based on the novel written by Patricia MacLachlan

Written by **Kathee Gosnell**
Illustrated by **Sue Fullam**

Teacher Created Materials, Inc.
6421 Industry Way
Westminster, CA 92683
www.teachercreated.com
©*1993 Teacher Created Materials, Inc.*
Reprinted, 2001
Made in U.S.A.
ISBN 1-55734-425-6

Table of Contents

Introduction

A good book can touch our lives like a good friend. Within its pages are words and characters that can inspire us to achieve our highest ideals. We can turn to it for companionship, recreation, comfort, knowledge, and guidance. It can make us laugh out loud, or cry at its tenderness. It can also give us a cherished story to hold in our hearts forever.

In *Literature Units,* great care has been taken to select books that are sure to become good friends!

Teachers who use this literature unit will find a special section for comparing and contrasting the selections. Teachers will discover the following features to supplement their own valuable ideas.

- Sample Lesson Plans

- Pre-reading Activities

- A Biographical Sketch and Picture of the Author

- Book Summaries

- Vocabulary Lists and Suggested Vocabulary Ideas

- Chapters grouped for study with each section including:
  - *a quiz*
  - *a hands-on project*
  - *a cooperative learning activity*
  - *cross-curricular connections*
  - *an extension into the reader's life*

- Post-reading Activities

- Book Report Ideas

- Research Ideas

- A Culminating Activity

- Three Options for Unit Tests

- A Bibliography

- An Answer Key

We are confident that this unit will be a valuable addition to your planning, and we hope that as you use our ideas, your students will increase the circle of "friends" they have in books!

Sample Lesson Plan

Each of the lessons suggested below can take from one to several days to complete. The lesson plan has been organized with the assumption that you will first have your students read *Sarah, Plain and Tall*. Then, do the activities in Sections 1 and 2. Next, read *Journey* and complete the activities in Sections 3 and 4. The activities in Section 5 focus on comparing and contrasting the two novels.

Lesson 1
- Introduce and complete some or all of the pre-reading activities on page 5.
- Read About the Author with your students. (page 6)
- Introduce the vocabulary list for Section 1. (page 9)

Lesson 2
- Read chapters 1 through 5 in *Sarah, Plain and Tall*. As you read, place the vocabulary words in the context of the story and discuss their meanings.
- Choose a vocabulary activity. (page 10)
- Make relief maps. (page 12)
- Compare and contrast hometowns. (page 13)
- Research material for Getting From Here to There and present reports to class. (page 14)
- Make dried flowers. (page 15)
- Administer the Section 1 quiz. (page 11)
- Introduce the vocabulary list for Section 2. (page 9)

Lesson 3
- Read chapters 6 through 9 in *Sarah, Plain and Tall*. Place the vocabulary words in context and discuss their meanings.
- Choose a vocabulary activity. (page 10)
- Have students learn a new skill. (page 17)
- Learn to barter. (page 18)
- Discuss the book in terms of art. (page 19)
- Begin Sarah's Diary. (page 20)
- Administer the Section 2 quiz. (page 16)
- Introduce the vocabulary list for Section 3. (page 9)

Lesson 4
- Read chapters 1 through 6 in *Journey*. Place the vocabulary words in context and discuss their meanings.
- Choose a vocabulary activity. (page 10)
- Continue Sarah's Diary. (page 20)
- Make a simple camera. (pages 22-23)
- Discuss the book in terms of its photographic history. Take photos and create a photo album based on a theme. (page 24)
- Write a want ad for *Journey*. (page 25)
- Discuss making changes in one's life. (page 26)
- Administer the Section 3 quiz. (page 21)
- Introduce the vocabulary list for Section 4. (page 9)

Lesson 5
- Read chapters 7 through 13 in *Journey*. Place the vocabulary words in context and discuss their meanings.
- Choose a vocabulary activity. (page 10)
- Complete Sarah's Diary. Share diary entries. (page 20)
- Plant a family tree. (page 28)
- Develop oral reading skills. (page 29)
- Listen to classical music. (page 30)
- Conduct a photo guessing contest. (page 31)
- Administer the Section 4 quiz. (page 27)
- Review vocabulary words. (page 9)

Lesson 6
- Use the quiz and activities in Section 5 to evaluate the students' knowledge and understanding of *Sarah, Plain and Tall* and *Journey*.
- Read summaries of both novels. (pages 7 and 8)
- Choose a vocabulary activity. (page 10)
- Make collage banners. (page 33)
- Write about and draw window scenes. (page 34)
- Scientifically categorize flowers. (page 35)
- Plan an imaginary journey. (page 36)
- Administer the Section 5 quiz. (page 32)

Lesson 7
- Discuss any questions your students may have about the stories. (page 37)
- Assign book reports and research projects. (pages 38 and 39)
- Begin work on the culminating activity. (pages 40-42)

Lesson 8
- Administer unit tests 1, 2, and/or 3. (pages 43-45)
- Discuss the test answers and responses.
- Discuss the students' opinions and enjoyment of the books.
- Provide a list of related reading for the students. (page 46)
- Celebrate the Family Reunion Culminating Activity.

Before the Book

Before you begin reading *Sarah, Plain and Tall* or *Journey*, provide students with information and materials that will create a better understanding of the time period and cultural framework in which each of the books is set.

In addition, try some of the following pre-reading activities to stimulate interest and help students focus on the literature.

1. Predict what the stories might be about by hearing the titles or looking at the cover illustrations.

2. Discuss prior knowledge that students might have about farming on the prairies, mail-order brides, living with one parent, the sea, fishing, photography, gardening, staying with grandparents on a farm, etc.

3. Discuss other books by Patricia MacLachlan that students may have heard or read about.

4. Discuss historical fiction.

5. Individually, or in small groups, make a time line. Be sure to include the period of time in which *Sarah, Plain and Tall* took place (approximately 1900) through the present (the approximate time period for *Journey*). Include on this time line significant events in your country's history.

6. Read actual accounts of pioneer homesteaders and photographers.

7. Answer these questions:

   Would you ever:

   —advertise in a newspaper or magazine for someone to come and live with you?

   —answer such an advertisement?

   —move into a environment that is totally different from your own?

   —move away from family and friends?

   —leave your children?

   —raise your grandchildren?

8. Write descriptions of what makes a person weak. Allow students to determine whether weakness is physical, emotional, psychological, or spiritual. Discuss their ideas.

About the Author

Patricia MacLachlan was born on March 3, 1938 to Philo and Madonna Pritzkau. "In a way," Mrs. MacLachlan said, "my childhood was one long bunch of pages...I read and read and read." She did not think, at age 8, that she would try to be a writer. But fortunately for her many fans, she began to write after her children were in school. Even though she was an only child, she writes books about brothers and sisters, about various types of families, and about loving, nurturing relationships. Because she was an only child, she spent a lot of time with her parents. Much of her material in her books comes from conversations she overheard between her parents and their friends. As a child, she studied the piano and then the cello. She continues to play chamber music with her husband and nearby friends.

Patricia MacLachlan was born in Cheyenne, Wyoming and raised in Minnesota. She loves to travel through the west and the plains. She said she needs to see and touch the prairie every so often.

On April 14, 1962, Patricia married Robert MacLachlan (a clinical psychologist). Also in 1962, she graduated from the University of Connecticut with a Bachelor of Arts degree. Robert and Patricia live with their three children, John, Jamie, and Emily in Williamsburg, Massachusetts—far from the western landscape that she claims has always been a powerful force in her life.

Before she began her writing career, Patricia was an English teacher. She served as a board member of the Children's Aid Family Service Agency from 1970-1980. In addition to writing, she teaches an introductory course on children's literature at Smith College in Massachusetts, goes into many classrooms to work with children, and is a visiting lecturer.

In 1979 Patricia published her first book, *The Sick Day.* She has written and published many more since. Her books have won many awards and honors. Patricia is perhaps best known for *Sarah, Plain and Tall,* which won the Newbery Medal in addition to numerous other honors. Several of her other books have also won awards.

Patricia MacLachlan offers this advice to students: "When I talked to students about writing, I stressed the importance of working every day. It helps hone your craft. But as I get older, I follow this advice less and less. My writing rhythm has 'peaks and valleys'. Sometimes we aren't meant to write and have to let our minds roam instead... Reading is absolutely crucial for a writer. Like children, we all learn by imitation... Books provide us with models, possibilities, inspiration, and courage. Reading is not a passive activity. Each time we read a book, we go on a journey. And as with all journeys, books change us and bring us back to our deeper selves."

(Quotations and information from *Something about the Author,* Gale Research, Volume 62.)

Sarah, Plain and Tall
by Patricia MacLachlan
(Harper & Row, 1987)
(Also available in Canada and Australia from Harper Collins and in U.K. from J. MacRae)

The day Caleb Witting is born, he is handed to his sister, Anna, in a yellow blanket. His mama thinks he is beautiful, but Anna considers him troublesome. She thinks he is homely and plain, and he has a terrible holler and a horrid smell. But the worst is yet to come—mama dies the next morning. Anna is left to be both mother and sister. Her resentment doesn't last more than three days. Caleb's smile warms and captivates her.

When he's old enough to talk, Caleb asks Anna about his mother every day. He is especially interested in the songs she used to sing. He knows his father used to sing, too. But Papa doesn't sing anymore. Anna doesn't remember the songs. Caleb thinks that if Anna could remember the songs, then he might remember his mama. When Caleb questions his father about the old songs, he replies: "I've forgotten the old songs, but maybe there's a way to remember them." He goes on to tell them that he has placed an advertisement in a newspaper for a wife, like their neighbor Matthew did when Maggie came to be his wife and a mother to his children.

Sarah Elizabeth Wheaton, from Maine, answers the ad. She and the Wittings get to know each other through letters. The day comes when Sarah announces that she will visit the Wittings to "see how it is." In a short letter Sarah writes, "I will come by train. I will wear a yellow bonnet. I am plain and tall." And at the bottom of the letter she adds, "Tell them I sing." Caleb can hardly wait. He wants so much for Sarah to like them all, even before he sees what she is like. It doesn't matter to him whether she is mild-mannered or not.

Sarah arrives with treasures from the sea, and her pet cat, Seal. So many things are different for Sarah that Anna and Caleb worry that perhaps she will soon long for the sea and the family she has left behind. Sarah is introduced to life on a farm on the prairie, so far from town that it is a day's journey there and back. Sarah pitches in to help however she can. Even when nature strikes a blow in the form of a squall, the pioneer family bounces back. Sarah's songs, and Sarah herself, endear the Witting family into wanting her to stay forever. Sarah discovers that even though she will always miss the sea, she would miss the family more. So she decides to stay.

Journey

by Patricia MacLachlan
(Delecorte Press, 1991)
*(Also available in Canada from Bantam Doubleday, in U.K from Bantam Dell, and in Australia from
Transworld Publishing)*

Eleven year old Journey and his sister, Cat, have been left by their mother, Liddie, to live with their
grandparents. Journey doesn't understand his mother's restlessness, but Liddie's parents knew her
departure was inevitable. Journey's father had gone away somewhere a long time ago. Now his father is
just a face on a photo, but the picture never told Journey the things he wanted to know. He searches
photo albums to find pictures of his family—his past. His grandma shows him a picture of his mother
as a girl, looking far off in the distance, and says, "Your mama always wished to be somewhere else."
When Liddie left, Journey's grandfather said, "She won't be back." Journey could not accept the
warning. When he searches to find pictures of his papa and mama and Cat and himself, his grandfather
tells him, "Your mama tore them up."

Journey is devastated. He takes to his bed until his sister, Cat, whips off his covers, pulls up the shades,
and tells him, "You're not sick, Journey, you're hiding out." He finally gets up and dresses. Grandma
comforts him with gentle words and hugs. Grandfather takes pictures—so many pictures that he drives
everyone to distraction. When he has an idea for a group family picture, everyone runs to different parts
of the house to hide. During one of these "vanishing scenes," Bloom, Journey's cat, finds torn pictures
in a box under Mama's bed. There are hundreds of tiny pictures, bits and pieces of faces, arms, and
bodies. Journey tries to piece them together. It's like a giant puzzle, but it becomes an impossible task.
Journey cannot piece together the ones he really wants. He finally gives up, admits to himself that his
mama is never coming back, and begins to get on with his life. He begins to get more involved with
photography with his grandfather. As time goes by, Journey realizes what his grandfather is doing with
all of his picture taking. After his grandfather develops the negatives of the torn pictures, Journey
discovers that the memories he associated with his papa were really memories of his grandfather. Now,
with his new-found knowledge, Journey can accept the love that has always bound his family
together—the love that was there all along.

Vocabulary Lists

On this page are vocabulary lists which correspond to each sectional grouping of chapters, as outlined in the Table of Contents on page 2. Vocabulary activity ideas can be found on page 10 of this book.

SECTION 1
(Chapters 1 through 5: *Sarah, Plain and Tall*)

hearthstones	holler	wretched	feisty
shuffling	energetic	pesky	wild-eyed
windbreak	flax	paddock	mica

SECTION 2
(Chapters 6 through 9: *Sarah, Plain and Tall*)

reins	tumbleweeds	petticoat	sputtering
whickering	primly	squall	pungent
nasturtiums	eerie	peering	squawk

SECTION 3
(Chapters 1 through 6: *Journey*)

rantry	dimwitted	unearthing	stills
sun-dappled	mingling	besotted	grainy
dialogue	shimmery	haughtily	banished
bureau	introspection	running-board	passenger pigeon

SECTION 4
(Chapters 7 through 13: *Journey*)

beckoned	tuckered	blotted	humane
twitch	compost	barren	clapboard
groused	tripod	wryly	motes
claque	chicory	rivulet	metronome

Vocabulary Activity Ideas

The first four sections contain several vocabulary words. You may wish to divide these words and assign them to small groups of students. The groups may define the words; find them in the context of the books, and present the information to the class to record in a vocabulary notebook.

You can help your students learn and retain the vocabulary in *Sarah, Plain and Tall* and *Journey* by providing them with interesting vocabulary activities. Here are a few ideas to try.

❑ Ask your students to make their own **Crosswords or Wordsearch Puzzles** using the vocabulary words from the novels.

❑ Challenge your students to a **Vocabulary Bee.** This is similar to a spelling bee, but in addition to spelling each word correctly, the game participants must correctly define the words.

❑ Have your students practice their writing skills by creating acrostics using each letter in a vocabulary word as the beginning letter in the first word of a sentence or phrase describing the word.

    Example: Cats are felines.

                Always like to clean themselves.

                Tabbies are kinds of cats.

❑ Ask your students to **write sentences or paragraphs** using as many vocabulary words as they possibly can.

❑ By using a generic spelling word game board, **play a board game** using the words in the vocabulary list. Make cards with a vocabulary word on a suitable-sized card. Put them on a draw pile. When a player lands on a draw square, they must give the definition for the drawn vocabulary word correctly or go back to start. This game can be played by any number of students at one time or teams during free time activities.

❑ Play **True or False.** Divide the class into 2 teams. Write vocabulary words on 1" x 2" (2.54 cm x 5 cm) cards. A vocabulary word is drawn from a hat (box, bag, etc.) by one team. A player on the opposite team must then give a definition. It can either be true or false. Then a player on the other team must decide if it's true or false. If correctly guessed, the team gets a point. Each player on the team gets a chance to give a definition and to guess. The team with the most points wins.

❑ Assign certain vocabulary words to the students. Have them put each one on a name card. They are to wear one each day attached to their clothing so it may easily be read by others. Whenever anyone in the classroom or throughout the school asks them what it is, they must **recite the word, its definition,** and use it in a sentence. Have them share the words with their families, too

❑ As a group activity, have students work together to create an **Illustrated Dictionary** of the vocabulary words.

❑ Play **Vocabulary Charades.** In this game, vocabulary words are acted out!

You probably have many more ideas to add to this list. Try them! Practicing selected words through these types of activities increases students' interest and retention of vocabulary.

                        10

Quiz

Answer the following questions about chapters 1 through 5 of *Sarah, Plain and Tall.*

1. On a separate sheet of paper list three major events of this section.

2. What questions does Caleb constantly ask Anna?

   _____

   _____

3. Why does Jacob place an advertisement in the newspapers for a wife?

   _____

   _____

4. What happens to the letters from Sarah?

   _____

   _____

5. When Sarah writes in a letter to Jacob that she is coming, what does she add at the bottom of the letter?

   _____

   _____

6. What do Anna and Caleb do while Papa goes to the train to get Sarah?

   _____

   _____

7. What does Sarah bring from the sea?

   _____

   _____

8. Why is Caleb excited when Sarah says she is going to pick flowers to dry, so that they can have flowers all winter long?

   _____

   _____

9. What does Anna think of Sarah?

   _____

   _____

10. How does Sarah react when a lamb dies?

   _____

   _____

Relief Maps

A relief map is a small-scale representation of a region. It is a special map because it shows the physical features of an area, such as mountains, plains, valleys, etc. These features may be represented by means of shading, contour lines, and colors on a two-dimensional surface. However, land features can be shown in three-dimensional form by using clay or other materials to represent them.

Find examples of relief maps in history books, atlases, and other reference books. Examine the ways in which features such as mountains and valleys are shown. After researching the materials and investigating land contours, put your research to work on the following activity.

Make a relief map showing the route Sarah might have taken from Maine to the prairie. You could also include the route that Maggie may have taken from Tennessee.

First you must decide how big your map will be. If you want to make it table-sized, you can form a small group with each member making one state, then fitting them together like a jigsaw puzzle. You could decide on a desk-sized model, and draw in the states you wish to represent.

Using a sturdy piece of cardboard as your base, pencil in an outline of your state or states. Next, make the dough you will use to show the contours of the land. Use the following materials and directions to help you complete your relief map.

Materials you will need:

- flour
- salt
- water
- bowl
- putty knife
- cardboard or poster board
- newspaper

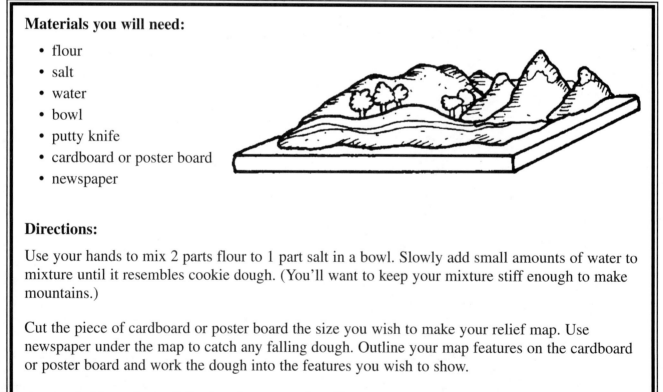

Directions:

Use your hands to mix 2 parts flour to 1 part salt in a bowl. Slowly add small amounts of water to mixture until it resembles cookie dough. (You'll want to keep your mixture stiff enough to make mountains.)

Cut the piece of cardboard or poster board the size you wish to make your relief map. Use newspaper under the map to catch any falling dough. Outline your map features on the cardboard or poster board and work the dough into the features you wish to show.

A putty knife works well for forming mountains. Use a putty knife or a table knife to make any main rivers you wish to include before the dough hardens. Your relief map should dry overnight, depending on the amount of moisture in the air. On the following day, you can paint your rivers, lakes, mountains, forest, railroad tracks, and/or whatever else you wish to add.

Compare and Contrast Hometowns

When Sarah responded to Jacob's advertisement, she wrote, "I have always loved to live by the sea, but at this time I feel a move is necessary. And the truth is, the sea is as far east as I can go." So Sarah went west approximately 1600 miles (2560 km) to a new life, a new environment.

Adopt an area that is about 1600 miles (2560 km) from your home, to be your new hometown. Then research the area you have chosen. Collect pictures, books, tourist information, etc. Maybe you can find some pen pals from your adopted area.

After you have gathered your material, make two lists. One list will be for entries from your home area. The other list is for entries from your adopted area.

Here are some categories you can use to compare and contrast your hometown from your adopted town.

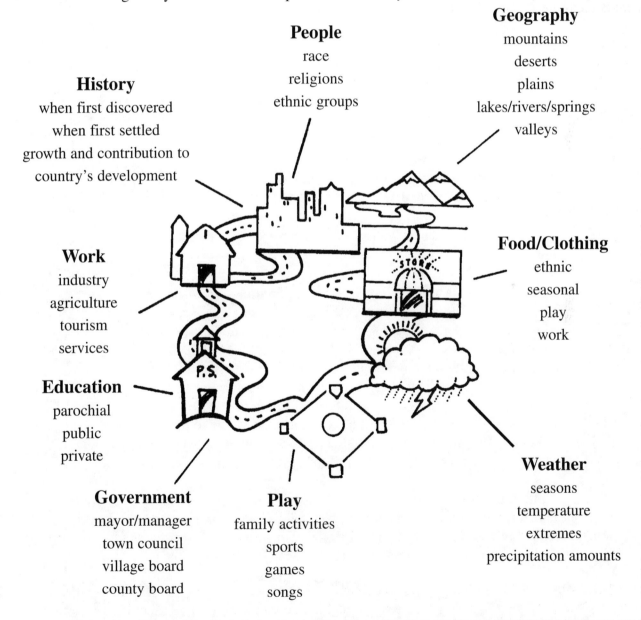

Geography
mountains
deserts
plains
lakes/rivers/springs
valleys

People
race
religions
ethnic groups

History
when first discovered
when first settled
growth and contribution to
country's development

Work
industry
agriculture
tourism
services

Food/Clothing
ethnic
seasonal
play
work

Education
parochial
public
private

Weather
seasons
temperature
extremes
precipitation amounts

Government
mayor/manager
town council
village board
county board

Play
family activities
sports
games
songs

Note to the teacher: Have the students include some comparable items noted in the story (e.g. swimming—pond vs. sea, sliding—haystack vs. dune, etc.)

Getting from Here to There

Sarah, Plain and Tall takes place in a pioneer prairie home on the frontier. Although the exact state location is not mentioned in the book, we know that Sarah's home state is Maine and that Maggie came from Tennessee.

Have the students break up into cooperative groups. Have some groups research the prairie states and decide which state they think would be an appropriate setting for the story. Also, have the groups determine what might have been the best route to get from Maine to that state.

Ask other groups to research railroads and report on the history of railroads. Have these groups map the railroad tracks from Maine and Tennessee to the prairie.

After completing their respective tasks, have each group report its findings to the class.

Trains were the fastest means of land transportation during the pioneer days, but they were slow according to today's standards. Mail often traveled on the trains. In *Sarah, Plain and Tall* we learned that it was a day's journey to the train station and back. From the information reported in the researched material, ask students to find out how long it would take for a letter to get to Sarah. Remind students that this information can be used to find out how long it would take for Sarah to get from Maine to the Wittings. Ask groups to solve related problems involving map distances and travel time.

Note to the teacher: In the TV movie adaptation of *Sarah, Plain and Tall,* it was noted that the story took place in Kansas in 1910. You may wish to use it as your setting.

Making Dried Flowers

Caleb is overjoyed when Sarah decides to pick flowers to dry. The family could then have flowers all winter long and be reminded of the sweet fragrances and natural beauty of spring and summer.

Make your own dried flowers to enjoy at home or give as a gift to someone special. The following method of air drying flowers is simple and inexpensive. You will have dried flowers for a bouquet or decoration in just a few weeks!

Materials: wild flowers or other fresh-cut flowers; nail, wire, string, or coat hanger; scissors; a warm, dry, clean, airy, dark place (for hanging flowers to dry)

Directions: Cut the flowers just before they are in full bloom and remove the leaves. Group flower families together, using a string or rubber band to tie their stems together. Be sure not to smash the blossoms tightly together because air must be able to circulate around the petals to dry the blossoms thoroughly in their original shape.

Hang the flower groupings upside-down, suspended from a nail, wire, string, or coat hanger. They will be dry in three to five weeks.

Quiz

Answer the following questions about chapters 6 through 9 of *Sarah, Plain and Tall.*

1. On a separate sheet of paper list 3 major events of this section.

2. Sarah asks Caleb and Anna to tell her about winter. They explain what it is like and what they do in winter. Make two columns on a separate sheet of paper. Under one, list how Caleb's and Anna's description is similar to where you live. Under the other column tell how the two places are different.

3. Who are Matthew and Maggie?

   _____

   _____

4. What things does Sarah tell Maggie that she misses?

   _____

   _____

5. What does Maggie tell Sarah in reply?

   _____

   _____

6. Why does Sarah put on Jacob's overalls?

   _____

   _____

7. What damages occur as a result of the storm?

   _____

   _____

8. Caleb thinks Sarah learned to ride too quickly. Why do Caleb and Anna cry about Sarah's desire to go away alone?

   _____

   _____

9. When Sarah returns from her excursion, she gives Anna and Caleb a package. Caleb is very excited. He says, "Sarah has brought the sea!" What is in the package?

   _____

   _____

10. On a separate sheet, write a paragraph describing what happens during the squall.

A Stitch in Time

During pioneer times, there was always plenty of work to do. Everyone in the family had chores. Boys usually helped their fathers, and girls helped their mothers. Sometimes everyone had to work on the same project. Sometimes boys and girls did chores other than those usually assigned to them, out of necessity or by choice.

In Sarah's letter to Anna she said, "Yes, I can braid hair and I can make stew and bake bread, though I prefer to build bookshelves and paint." Later she helped plow the fields and fix the roof. Jacob, too, was used to doing "women's work."

Take a poll in your classroom. How many boys bake bread, biscuits, cookies, or cakes? How many girls make woodworking projects such as bird houses, toy boxes, etc.? Get into the pioneer spirit and try a project or chore that you might never have considered doing before. If you've never baked before, try a simple recipe for a food you really enjoy. If you've never made things out of wood, try your hand at making a birdhouse or a woodworking project.

You could be a great help at home by learning to repair holes in your clothes. One way to repair holes in material is by darning. Practice darning a torn sock using the directions below.

Directions for Darning a Sock:

1. Thread a needle with a double length of thread. Knot the ends.

2. Drop a "darning egg" into the sock. This is an object that holds the shape of the sock while you are mending. A small plastic ball like a ping-pong ball works nicely.

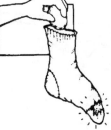

3. Stitch across the hole from left to right, keeping your stitches snug over the darning egg.

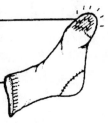

4. Stitch across the hole from top to bottom, keeping your stitches snug over the darning egg and left-to-right stitches.

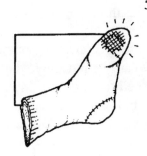

5. Knot your last stitch and cut the thread. Your sock is ready to wear!

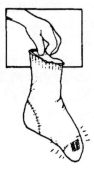

Time to Barter

Matthew and Maggie came to help Jacob plow a new field for corn. "Papa needs five horses for the big gang plow," Caleb told Sarah. "Prairie grass is hard."

Neighbors quite often combined efforts to get certain chores, or undertakings accomplished quicker, easier, and more efficiently. Jacob could not afford to feed and house five horses all year long when two horses was all he normally needed. He probably used a smaller plow on the fields that had been tilled before. It is very unlikely that Jacob had a big gang plow. Instead, Matthew would have to take his plow and horses to help Jacob. People could not always afford to pay cash for the help, so they would barter. Barter means to trade, or exchange goods or services without using money. This is how neighbors would help each other.

Harvesting was a time when neighbors got together to help one another. If it was time for haying, or threshing, or corn picking, neighbors would work together by combining machinery, animals, or whatever was needed to get the job done. They would go from farm to farm until the same job was done on each farm. Men, women, and children would pitch in to help. If you didn't help in the field, you helped get food ready to feed everyone.

Work was made lighter when everyone helped. You may have heard the expression, "Many hands make light work." These neighborly gatherings also became social occasions, time to visit and catch up on the latest gossip. Barn and house raising was another time that neighbors would get together to help.

Sometimes people would barter skills that they had for skills they lacked or didn't have time to do. A blacksmith might exchange services with a carpenter. A doctor might provide services for a seamstress, who in return, might repair or make new clothing for the doctor. A teacher might exchange services with a cook, and so on.

Think about the skills or special talents you may have. What are you particularly good at? It does not have to be something requiring a specific skill like sewing, or cooking, or building, or painting. Perhaps you are especially good at cleaning up or organizing things, mowing the lawn, washing the car.

Decide what you could possibly do for someone else, like cleaning out a desk or locker for a classmate, mowing a neighbor's lawn, or washing the family car. Then decide what you would want in return. Remember this is bartering and no cash is exchanged for services! Make a small poster announcing your proposition. Post it on a classroom or school bulletin board or at your local Senior Citizen's Center. Mowing lawns or washing dishes in exchange for a batch of homemade cookies made by a member of the Senior Citizen's Center sounds like a delicious way to barter. You might hear some fascinating stories from the past as well, and develop new friendships. Don't forget to report to your classmates on your success and/or failures.

Pictures Worth a Thousand Words

One of the things that Sarah preferred to do was to draw pictures. She drew pictures to send home to her brother William. Make a booklet containing pictures that Sarah might have drawn Don't be concerned if they are not perfect—remember, Sarah drew a sheep whose ears were too big. The important thing is to have fun.

In the frame below, draw a picture or cut the framed picture out and display it along with drawings made by other students. Or, combine all drawings into a class book using some of the following items or characters mentioned in the story.

- a charcoal drawing of the fields
- a sheep whose ears are too big
- a windmill
- Papa, his hair curly and full of hay

- Caleb, sliding down the hay, his arms over his head
- Anna in the tub, her hair long and straight and wet
- a picture of Sarah's sea (blue and gray and green)

Note to the teacher: Pictures can also be added from *Journey* (either drawings or photos). The booklets can be put on display during Family Reunion.

Sarah's Diary

Do you keep a diary? Many people do. You would be surprised by how easily we forget everyday occurrences. It is fun reading entries made in a diary months or years later. Many pioneers kept diaries. Our history of the settling of America was made more complete and interesting by diaries handed down from generation to generation.

It is time to put your imagination to work. Pretend that you are Sarah and that you have kept a diary for many years. Record a week's worth of thoughts and feelings as Sarah begins her adventure on the prairie. By using the major events in *Sarah, Plain and Tall*, you can find plenty of things to write about. Remember to include Sarah's emotions as she reacted to the events. Tell about the things she disliked as well as the changes in her life that she enjoyed.

Here are some of the events you could write about:

the train ride to the prairie	the trip from train to farm
Jacob, Anna, Caleb	the farm
flower picking	singing
sheep	hay mound/dune
pictures to William	plowing
the chickens	swimming in the cow pond
the flower garden	Matthew, Maggie, Rose, Violet
the storm	fixing the house roof
riding Old Bess	driving the wagon
bringing the sea home to everyone	

- -

Note to the teacher: This activity could be combined with the Curriculum Connections activity, Pictures Worth a Thousand Words on page 19. A drawing could be made on one page with its diary entry on the adjacent page.

Quiz

Answer the following questions about chapters 1 through 6 of *Journey*.

1. On a separate sheet of paper list three major events of this section.

2. Where does Journey's grandfather get the camera?

   _____

   _____

3. How does Journey react when he receives his first letter from his mama and discovers that it holds only money?

   _____

   _____

4. How does Journey feel, at first, when his grandfather takes pictures of him?

   _____

   _____

5. Grandma and Journey are looking at old pictures in an album. Journey sees pictures and thinks they are nice except for the picture of his mama. He blames it on the camera. What is his grandma's reply?

   _____

   _____

6. Who is Cooper?

   _____

   _____

7. What is the first picture that Journey takes of his grandfather?

   _____

   _____

8. When Journey comments that the picture he took of Grandfather and Emmett isn't perfect, what does Grandfather reply?

   _____

   _____

9. What had happened to Journey's baby pictures and pictures of Cat, his mama, and his papa?

   _____

   _____

10. Why does Cat chase Journey out of his bed?

    _____

    _____

A Simple Camera

Grandfather and Journey used a camera to take candid pictures of everyday events in their lives. Here is your opportunity to make a camera that actually works.

Materials you will need:

- coffee can (with plastic lid)
- black construction paper
- glue
- waxed paper
- rubber band
- small nail
- newspaper

- hammer
- black electrical tape
- photographic paper
- scissors
- coat or blanket
- paper tape

Directions:

1. Turn the coffee can upside-down on a desk or table that has been covered with newspaper. Mark the center point of the bottom of the can.

2. Place the nail tip on the center point. Use a hammer to punch a small pinhole in the bottom of the can.

3. Cut a piece of waxed paper large enough to fit around and hang over the can opening. Place the waxed paper over the opening and secure it with a rubber band. Make sure the waxed paper is smooth and tight.

4. Your coffee can camera is now ready to use. See page 23 for instructions on how to hold the camera and take real pictures.

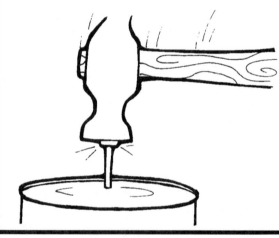

A Simple Camera *(cont.)*

It takes a little practice but on a sunny day you can actually see an image formed through the pinhole. Hold the camera in front of your eyes with the waxed paper end closest to you. (See step 4 on page 22.) Face the pinhole end toward a bright object in a sunny area. Put a blanket or coat over your head and the part of the coffee can nearest you. Keep your eyes about 8" to 12" (20 cm to 30 cm) away from the can. As you point the can towards a bright object, the object will project onto the waxed paper—upside down.

If you wish to take pictures, you will need to attach some photosensitive material to the cover of the coffee can. First prepare the can lid. Cut a circle from black construction paper to the exact diameter of the inside of the coffee can lid. Glue the paper inside the lid. The photosensitive material that's best to use in one of these cameras is photographic paper. Under safe light in a darkroom, the paper to be exposed in the camera should be placed inside the coffee can lid. The light-sensitive side should face out. The sensitive side of photographic paper is the shiny side. Cut your paper to fit the cover as best as you can. Double a piece of paper tape back on itself to keep the paper in place while moving it about.

The shutter is made from a piece of black tape placed over the pinhole with a little handle created on one side so that it can be easily grasped. Exposures are made by simply removing the tape for the length of the exposure and then replacing it. You can do several experiments by timing the length the shutter is open.

The most common cause for failure in making photographs with a pinhole camera is a light leak in the camera, so be sure your cover fits tightly. You may have to place black tape around the seam if any gaps occur.

After you have recorded your image in your camera, you will want to process your photograph and make prints. If your school has a darkroom, make arrangements to get it developed there. Or perhaps a local photographer can help you. It is most important to keep the light from leaking in from the shutter or the cover, so handle your camera with extreme care.

You can be creative and decorate your camera to make it unique. You will want to put your camera on display during Family Reunion, along with any prints you have developed. Smile and say Cheese!

Say Cheese!

A pinhole camera is a box with a pinhole at one end and film at the other end. It is the simplest kind of camera. You can let light shine through the hole and onto the film.

But a pinhole camera cannot take pictures of things that move fast, or objects in a dim light, or things that are too close. To take all these kinds of pictures, a camera must have more parts.

Use books from your school or local library that have information on cameras, the history of the camera, and camera parts and their functions. Identify the parts of the camera below using the following terms. Then, write the definitions of each term on the line next to it.

lens _____

shutter _____

diaphragm _____

viewfinder _____

film knob _____

If possible, bring a camera to school. If the school has a camera, perhaps your class can borrow it. Next, plan a photo album using a series of specific pictures. Choose a theme around which you will center your photographs and be sure your pictures reflect the theme. Add a caption to each photograph. Organize the photos into the photo album you have created. Share your album with the class.

Want Ad

In *Sarah, Plain and Tall,* Jacob wrote an advertisement for a mail-order bride. Think about what he may have said in the advertisement.

Journey's Mama left the year Journey was eleven. Grandfather warned Journey that Mama would not return. The relationship between Journey and his mother was far from "ideal." Journey probably thought often about what it would be like if the situation was different—if Mama was there for him.

Imagine that Journey wrote an advertisement for a mail-order mom. What qualities do you think Journey would wish for in a mother? Pretend you are searching for a mother or father. What qualities in a person are important to you? What type of person are you looking for? The more information you include in your ad, the better your chances are for finding the ideal mother or father.

When you have considered the information you would like to include in your advertisement, fill in the Want Ad below.

Cat Relinquishes

Cat gave Grandfather the camera in one of her fits of cleanliness. "I've given up the camera," she yelled, her head beneath the bed, unearthing her life. "I've given up the flute and most everything else. Including meat," she said pointedly. "I have spent the entire afternoon looking into the eyes of a cow, and have become a vegetarian."

We all have probably done something similar to what Cat did. That is, we started some book, project, hobby, task, intention, ambition, or plan, but for some reason or another, let it gather dust on a shelf or under the bed. Life is fraught with change. We're constantly trying out new ideas. That's how we develop our ideals and our ideology.

On a sheet of paper, list as many similar items that you've given up on as you can. Choose two or three items to elaborate upon. Explain how you would do them differently if you were to do them over. Have you made any conscious changes in your life, such as Cat did by becoming a vegetarian, including those in which you've made your own decisions, without family influence or pressure? Explain why you made these changes.

Quiz

Answer the following questions about chapters 7 through 13 of *Journey*.

1. On a separate sheet of paper, list three major events of this section.

2. Who is Bloom?

   _____

   _____

3. What does Grandma think of Bloom?

   _____

   _____

4. Who finds the torn pictures? Where were the pictures?

   _____

   _____

5. What does Journey intend to do with the pictures? Why?

   _____

   _____

6. When does Journey realize his mama is never coming back?

   _____

   _____

7. On a separate sheet of paper, write a paragraph describing a little about the MacDougals.

8. After Journey talks to Grandfather about his phone conversation with his mama, they look at some of the family pictures. Journey makes Grandfather laugh. Why does Journey feel the urge to kiss him?

   _____

   _____

9. Into what does Grandfather turn the barn tool room?

   _____

   _____

10. What does Journey discover when Grandfather develops the negatives of Mama's pictures?

   _____

   _____

Family Tree

Throughout the story, Journey struggles with the sadness and anger caused when his mother leaves him and his sister, Cat, with their grandparents. At the end of the story, Journey discovers that Grandfather was always a part of his past. It was his papa's face he didn't know—didn't remember. Through the photos, Grandfather was creating a history for him.

Genealogy is a recorded history of the descent of a person or family from an ancestor or ancestors. It is the study of family ancestries and histories—tracing lineage.

Perhaps you are familiar with family trees. A family tree is a method used to connect a person with his/her ancestors. Here is a sample using the information available in our story.

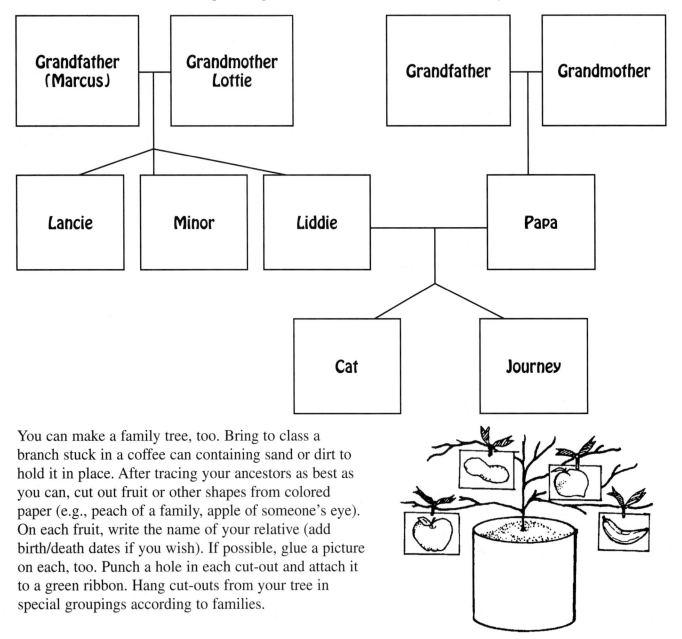

You can make a family tree, too. Bring to class a branch stuck in a coffee can containing sand or dirt to hold it in place. After tracing your ancestors as best as you can, cut out fruit or other shapes from colored paper (e.g., peach of a family, apple of someone's eye). On each fruit, write the name of your relative (add birth/death dates if you wish). If possible, glue a picture on each, too. Punch a hole in each cut-out and attach it to a green ribbon. Hang cut-outs from your tree in special groupings according to families.

- -

Note to the teacher: Decide beforehand how big the branches should be and how far back the families should be traced.

Trot, Trot to Boston

Baby Emmett was happy and excited to see Grandfather. Grandfather probably played games like Trot, Trot to Boston with him before. Later in the story, Journey remembers it was Grandfather who sang Trot, Trot to Boston to him. It was his grandfather's knees, not Papa's knees he sat upon.

Babies love rhymes, songs, and poems. They love the repetition and familiarity of their favorites. Favorite poems, songs, and books stay with a person forever. They are passed on from generation to generation. This is not something new. Before books were readily available, storytelling was a favorite pastime for a very long time.

Here is your chance to instill the love of literature in someone else. Make arrangements with a nearby nursery school or kindergarten to "adopt" a little girl or boy as your storytelling partner. Choose a nursery rhyme, short story, poem, or song to share with your partner. Become familiar with it. Memorize it, if possible. Practice at home and at school with your classmates. Story telling is more than reading aloud. Use body language to help make it more interesting. Use your voice to express feelings that you want to convey to your partner.

Set up several appointments to meet with your partner. Encourage him/her to learn your selection so that after awhile, he/she can repeat part or all of it to you. The more you enjoy what you are doing, the more your partner will enjoy it. So have fun!

Concert Time!

Two months had gone by, but it did not seem that long to Journey. The kittens were half grown, Emmett was learning to talk, and Grandma had made it through an entire song, from beginning to end, on the flute. She said it was her version of Vivaldi.

Antonio Vivaldi was an Italian composer (1678-1741). He was one of the most productive composers of the elaborately rhythmic and melodic music called "baroque music." Vivaldi wrote nearly 50 operas, much church music, and hundreds of concertos for almost every instrument known at the time.

Grandma was practicing Vivaldi on the porch surrounded by her claque of cats. Now it is concert time! Weather permitting, take the class outside to sit in the grass or perhaps take students to a nearby bandshell. On a cassette recorder, play a Vivaldi concerto or other available works for the group to listen to. Or better still, get your school's band teacher or one of his/her students to play some Vivaldi pieces on a flute like Grandma did.

As the children listen, have them imagine that they are sitting on the porch with Grandma and the cats. Let their imaginations conjure up images of what the music is telling them. Have them describe what is happening to them and around them, as they sit on Grandma's porch. But most of all enjoy the beautiful music!

Illustrate or write about your images and share them with the class.

Who's That Baby?

Journey discovered family resemblances as he came across photographs in albums and picture frames. Cat looked like her Mama and Grandma. Journey looked like his grandfather. Journey's friend, Cooper, and his brother, Emmett, look alike. "We all look alike," said Cooper. "The whole family, down through the ages, over prairie and sea, desert and mountain. You could toss all our pictures up in the air, and when they came down they'd all look like me."

Do you look most like a brother or sister, mother, father, aunt, uncle, grandma, grandpa, or cousin?

If possible, bring to class a photo of the relative you resemble most. Try to get a picture of when they were at the same age you are now. Also, bring to class a photo of yourself when you were a baby or a toddler. Put your name on the back of each photo for easy identification.

After all the pictures are assembled, your teacher can put them up randomly on a bulletin board. Assign each picture a number. Now for the fun part. Hold a contest. Try to match the most photos of each classmate to his or her relative.

- -

Note to the teacher: Offer a prize for the winner. Perhaps you can get a local photography studio to give a free family portrait or provide one at a nominal fee.

Quiz

Answer the following questions about *Sarah, Plain and Tall* and *Journey* by comparing and contrasting the people and events in the two stories.

1. On a separate sheet of paper, list three similarities between the lives of Anna and Caleb and Cat and Journey.

2. On a separate sheet of paper, list three differences between the lives of Anna and Caleb and Cat and Journey.

3. Both Caleb and Journey are searching for something in their stories. What is each searching for?

   _____

   _____

4. Sarah and Journey had similar reactions of anger and sadness over incidents that caused worry and concern from family and friends. What happened to Sarah that caused her reaction? Journey?

   _____

   _____

5. What does Sarah do after she finds the lamb that had been killed?

   _____

   _____

6. What is Journey's reaction to his discovery that his mama tore up the family pictures?

   _____

   _____

7. In *Journey*, Grandfather and then Journey would take spontaneous pictures of the family. What spontaneous thing did Sarah and the Wittings do?

   _____

   _____

8. In *Sarah, Plain and Tall*, Maggie offers words of wisdom to Sarah that Sarah later uses as her own. What were they?

   _____

   _____

9. Grandfather similarly offers words of wisdom to Journey—words that he later uses. What were they?

   _____

   _____

10. What discoveries did Sarah and Journey make at the end of their stories?

   _____

   _____

Collage Banners

A good story does not need pictorial images to hold your attention. A well written story will entice mental images to keep your interest while you're reading through well developed imagery.

What images do you bring to mind when you think of *Sarah, Plain and Tall*? The farm? Animals? Flowers?

What images form as you think about *Journey*? Cameras? Photographs? Cats and Kittens?

Make a list of what you imagine as you think about the stories. Next, try to find some pictures in old magazines, etc., that would closely fit those images.

Form a small group and trace and cut out large letters spelling the words "*Sarah, Plain and Tall*" and "*Journey.*" Then, take the pictures that have been gathered and paste or glue them onto the letters.

Don't worry about overlapping the letters or the pictures. Fill up all of the letters with pictures, then trim them to their proper letter shapes. Next, staple, pin, or glue the letters onto long strips of cloth slightly larger than your letters. (Perhaps a family member can donate an old sheet to be torn or cut into the needed strips.) Finally, hang the banners across your classroom. Step back and enjoy your colorful banners.

Window Scenes

In *Sarah, Plain and Tall*, Anna looked out her window. This is what she saw: "Outside, the prairie reached out and touched the places where the sky came down. Though winter was nearly over, there were patches of snow and ice everywhere. I looked at the long dirt road that crawled across the plains..."

Journey closed his eyes and could see the farm... "the spruce trees at the edge of the meadow, the stream cutting through, the stone walls that framed it all. I knew every inch of every acre."

The author, Patricia MacLachlan, "paints" these pictures with well-chosen words. The reader is able to visualize what both Anna and Journey could see.

Write a paragraph describing what you see out your favorite window. Use descriptive words to "paint" a perfect picture. Now read it to a partner. Then have your partner read his/her paragraph to you. Separate. Using colored pencils, crayons, or paints, draw your partner's window scene in the window frame below. "Paint" your picture using the written words from your partner's paragraph. After everyone has completed the pictures, hang them up around the room. Now see if you can identify which window is yours.

Flowers-Flowers-Flowers!

Now it is time for all you blooming botanists to categorize all those flowers mentioned in the two stories.

If possible, gather samples of live flowers, or find pictures to cut out, or draw and color your own. This activity can be done individually or in groups. Research some of the flowers common to your area or choose among those mentioned in the book. Make Botany Books complete with the scientific names of your flowers, illustrations, and common locations of the flowers. Add dried flower samples to your Botany Book using the flowers you have prepared from page 15. Check your library for plant and wild flower books that will give you that information.

Here is a partial listing of the flowers mentioned in each story:

Sarah, Plain and Tall

Indian PaintBrush	Columbine	Blue-Eyed Grass
Nasturtiums	Blue Flax	Pansy
Clover	Prairie Violets	Wild Roses
Bride's Bonnet	Wild Asters	Seaside Goldenrod
Woolly Ragwort	Dandelions	Wild Daisies
Zinnias	Marigolds	Wild Feverfew
	Dahlias	

Journey

Mountain Laurel	Lilacs	Lily-of-the-Valley
Hollyhocks	Peonies	Petunias
Red Salvia	Wild Chicory	Queen Anne's Lace
	Bee Balm	

Journey's Journey

"Mama named me Journey. Journey, as if somehow she wished her restlessness on me." This is how Patricia MacLachlan begins the story of Journey. Journey is aptly named, not only because of his mama's restlessness, but also because he experiences a journey of personal growth and maturity within himself.

When his mama leaves, Journey lashes out and hits his grandfather. Grandfather knew Journey's mama would go and would not be back and he said so. Then Journey's journey begins. He finally accepts what his mother did as inevitable and that his grandparents and sister Cat were his family—a family that loved him and was ready to stand by him.

Caleb, in *Sarah, Plain and Tall* also had a journey of his own. Since his mother died the day after he was born, he longed for someone to take her place. He readily accepted Sarah, but had to wait for a bond to develop between them. His journey seemed agonizingly slow as Sarah grew to accept and love everyone and everything on their farm.

Here is an opportunity for you to take a journey of your own. Imagine that you are Journey. You have invented a time machine. Caleb is one of your ancestors. You decide to go back in time to visit him. You want to take with you three items that would make Caleb's life easier. Discuss with a partner what items you would take with you and why you chose each.

On your return trip, Caleb gives you three items to remember him by. In the time machines below, illustrate the items you think Caleb would give you. On index cards tell why he might have chosen each. Cut out the time machines. Glue the time machines and index cards onto a piece of construction paper. Display or share with the class.

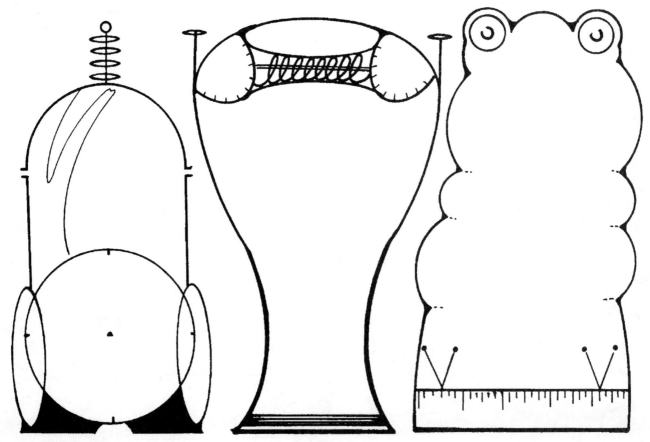

Any Questions?

When you finished reading *Sarah, Plain and Tall* and/or *Journey*, did you have some questions that were left unanswered? Write some of your questions here.

_____

_____

_____

_____

_____

Work in groups or by yourself to prepare possible answers for some or all of the questions you have asked above and those written below. When you have finished your predictions, share your ideas with the class.

- What happens to Sarah? Does she marry Jacob? Does she have children of her own? Does she ever go back to her old home again? Do her brother and his family ever come for a visit?

- If Sarah has her own children, do Anna and Caleb accept them gladly into the family? Do Anna and Caleb ever visit the sea with Sarah? Do they grow up and stay in the area and raise their own families? Does Caleb sing for his children? Does he become a farmer or a fisherman?

- Do Matthew and Maggie remain neighbors? Do they play an important role in Sarah's life? Does Caleb marry Rose or Violet? Do Maggie and Matthew have children of their own that play with Sarah's children?

- Do they have any more tragedies in their lives? Does Sarah become mild mannered? Will progress change their way of living?

- Does Liddie ever come back to see Cat and Journey? Does their papa ever come back in their lives? Do Cat and Journey ever live with their mother again?

- Do Cat and Cooper get married? If so, where do they live? What do they do? Do they have children? What kind of parents will they be?

- What happens to Journey? Does he always remain in the area? Does he continue with photography? Does he get married and raise a family? Does he play Trot, Trot to Boston with his children? Does he get restless like Liddie and "take off"?

- What happens to Marcus and Lottie? Do they continue with their hobbies? Do they try to find Liddie or the children's papa?

Book Report Ideas

There are many ways to report on a book once it has been read. After you have finished *Sarah, Plain and Tall* and *Journey,* choose a method of reporting on it that appeals to you. It may be an idea of your own or one of the suggestions mentioned below.

- **Eye Can Visualize**

  By using arts and crafts you are familiar and comfortable with, construct a model of a scene from either story, a drawing or a sculpture of a likeness of one or more of the characters, or craft an important symbol from the book as a visual report.

- **Time Capsule**

  Provide people in the future with reasons to read *Sarah, Plain and Tall* or *Journey.* Inside a time capsule-shaped design, neatly write your reasons. You may "bury" the capsule after you have shared it with your class.

- **Lights! Camera! Action!**

  A size-appropriate group can prepare a scene from either story for dramatization, act it out, and relate the significance of the scene to the entire book. Add costumes and props to set the stage. Record it on videotape so everyone can see the production.

- **The Sequel**

  Many of you have probably seen movie sequels or read sequels to favorite books. What would *Sarah, Plain and Tall* and *Journey* be like if the stories continued? Predict what might happen. You may write it as a story in a narrative form, a dramatic script, or do a visual display.

- **Twenty Clues or Less**

  Give a series of clues about a character from either story in a general to a specific order. After each clue, have someone in the class try to guess the character. After all of the clues are given, if the subject cannot be guessed, the reporter may tell the class. The reporter then does the same for an event in the book and then for an important object or symbol.

- **Sales Talk**

  Create an advertisement to "sell" *Sarah, Plain and Tall* or *Journey* to one or more specific groups. You decide on the group to target and the sales pitch you will use. Include some kind of graphics in your presentations.

- **Coming Attraction**

  Sarah, Plain and Tall has already been made into a movie. Now you have been chosen to make *Journey* into one. Design the promotional poster. Include the title and author of the book, a listing of the main characters and the contemporary actors who will play them, a drawing of a scene from the book, and a paragraph synopsis of the story that will make audiences want to see the movie.

- **Talk Show Interviews**

  This can be done by any size group. One student will play a talk show host. The host will read off questions from a list prepared by the guests (characters from either story). The guests will answer the questions asked them by the host, trying to provide the audience with the insights into the character's personality and life that the audience most wants to know.

Research Ideas

Describe three things that you read in *Sarah, Plain and Tall* and *Journey* that you would like to learn more about.

Sarah, Plain and Tall

1. _____
2. _____
3. _____

Journey

1. _____
2. _____
3. _____

As you read *Sarah, Plain and Tall,* you encountered several geographic locations, true-life people and events, pioneer customs and lifestyles, ways of speaking, colloquialisms, songs, struggles with nature, and more that require some background knowledge to make the reading more meaningful. To increase your understanding of the characters and events of the book, and to appreciate Patricia MacLachlan's craft as a writer, research to find out more about these people, places, and things.

Do the same for *Journey* as you work in groups to research one or more of the areas you named above or the areas that are listed below. Share your findings with the rest of the class in any appropriate format for oral presentation.

- train travel
- Pioneer
  - homes
  - education
  - home life & families
  - clothing
  - cooking
  - farming
  - celebrations/songs
  - flowers
- the sea
- horses/wagons
- cats/kittens
- seasons in Maine/prairie
- cameras
- stone walls
- flutes
- passenger pigeons
- blueberry barren
- farm/country
  - chores
  - equipment
  - cooking
  - animals

- mail-order brides
- whales
- sea birds
- seals
- Maine
- Tennessee
- the prairie
- swimming
- fishing/fishing boats
- birds' nests
- dunes
- photography equipment
- spruce trees
- Vivaldi
- gardens
- metronome
- older models of cars with huge fenders, running boards and stick shifts

Family Reunion

If you have ever been to a family reunion, you know the one question that is frequently asked is, "Whose child are you?" Since everyone is family, the questioner wants to know your family tree. Are you Jacob's boy? Sarah's girl? Lottie's sister? Marcus's brother? Your answer would depend on whose side of the family you're getting together with, your mother's or your father's side of the family.

Let's link our two selections, *Sarah, Plain and Tall*, and *Journey* together by making the characters of *Sarah, Plain and Tall* into the ancestors of the characters in *Journey*. Get together in small groups and trace the lineage of Journey. Make an outline of a tree, similar to the one below, using construction paper. Then add the appropriate information to complete the lineage of Journey. Feel free to expand on the tree. Make up names or characters that were not mentioned in the selections. Then elect a group spokesperson to share your ideas with the class. As a class, choose which tree you will "adopt" as an appropriate family tree. Use the example below to help you plan your family tree.

Example:

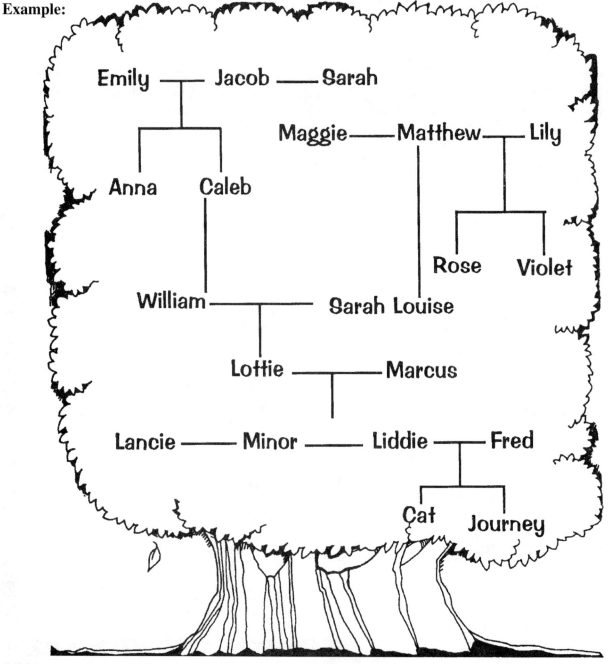

Family Reunion *(cont.)*

Now that you have established your family tree, it is time to plan a family reunion. Here is your chance to show your family what you have been studying. Introduce your family to the families in our selections.

To plan your classroom Family Reunion, get into small groups again. Brainstorm your ideas to plan the day's events. Decide who to invite, what to do, what to display, the order of events for the day, and what needs to be done to get ready. When each group has completed its brainstorming session, the group spokesperson will share his/her ideas with the class. As a class, choose the events and displays you will have for your day.

If you wish to invite parents, siblings, grandparents, etc., use the invitation at the top of page 42. Fill out and distribute the name tags on the bottom of page 42 to invited guests. Don't forget to wear one yourself.

Here are some ideas for the displays and events for your Family Reunion.

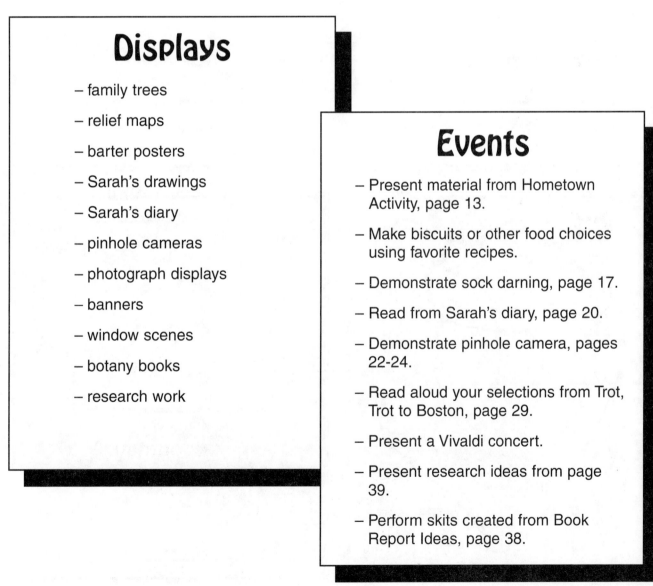

Displays

- family trees
- relief maps
- barter posters
- Sarah's drawings
- Sarah's diary
- pinhole cameras
- photograph displays
- banners
- window scenes
- botany books
- research work

Events

- Present material from Hometown Activity, page 13.
- Make biscuits or other food choices using favorite recipes.
- Demonstrate sock darning, page 17.
- Read from Sarah's diary, page 20.
- Demonstrate pinhole camera, pages 22-24.
- Read aloud your selections from Trot, Trot to Boston, page 29.
- Present a Vivaldi concert.
- Present research ideas from page 39.
- Perform skits created from Book Report Ideas, page 38.

Family Reunion *(cont.)*

Provide an appropriate number of copies of this page for each student to complete the culminating activity described on pages 40 and 41.

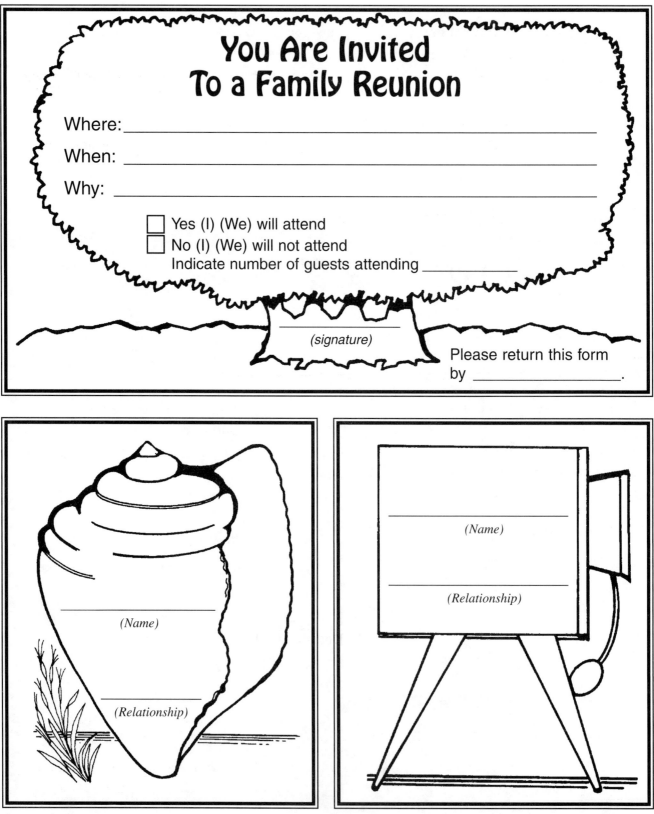

You Are Invited To a Family Reunion

Where: _____

When: _____

Why: _____

☐ Yes (I) (We) will attend
☐ No (I) (We) will not attend
Indicate number of guests attending _____

_____
(signature)

Please return this form by _____.

_____
(Name)

_____
(Relationship)

_____
(Name)

_____
(Relationship)

Unit Test

Matching: Match the descriptions of the characters with their names. Place the letter of the correct choice on the line next to the character.

Sarah, Plain and Tall

1._____	Jacob Witting	A. is not mild mannered
2._____	Anna Witting	B. went with Sarah to town
3._____	Caleb Witting	C. placed an advertisement in the newspapers for a wife
4._____	Sarah Wheaton	D. aunts and lambs
5._____	William Wheaton	E. came to help plow a new field for corn
6._____	Matthew & Maggie	F. hooted and laughed and chased chickens and dogs
7._____	Rose & Violet	G. thought he was loud and pesky
8._____	Old Bess & Jack	H. a fisherman with a boat called Kittiwake
9._____	Lottie & Nick	I. loved Sarah first
10._____	Harriet, Mattie, Lou	J. dreamed a perfect dream that Sarah was happy

Journey

1._____	Journey	A. parents own a fruit stand
2._____	Cat	B. a photographer and farmer
3._____	Liddie	C. an 11 year old boy abandoned by his mother
4._____	Mary Louise	D. a woman who always wished to be somewhere else
5._____	Marcus	E. found the torn pictures under Mama's bed
6._____	Cooper MacDougal	F. spent entire afternoon looking into eyes of a cow and became a vegetarian
7._____	Emmett MacDougal	G. played Vivaldi on the flute
8._____	Lottie	H. besotted with Cat
9._____	Millie Bender	I. untrustworthy cow
10._____	Bloom	J. rode in a sling like a baby chimpanzee

True or False: Answer true or false in the blanks below.

1.	_____	Sarah came in the summer.
2.	_____	Sarah missed the sea, William, and the aunts.
3.	_____	Jacob didn't know why Sarah went to town alone.
4.	_____	Cat was glad to get the money her mother sent.
5.	_____	Mr. MacDougal kissed Journey on his forehead.
6.	_____	Journey's parents finally came for him.

Essay: Answer the following on the back of this paper.

1. Maggie sympathized with Sarah's loneliness. She said, "There are always things to miss, no matter where you are." Explain what these words meant to Maggie, Sarah, and Anna.

2. Grandfather makes a statement, "A thing doesn't have to be perfect to be fine. That goes for a picture. That goes for life. Things can be good enough." Explain what this meant to Journey.

Response

Explain the meaning of these quotations from *Sarah, Plain and Tall* and *Journey*.

Note to the teacher: Choose an appropriate number of quotes to which your students should respond.

Sarah, Plain and Tall

Chapter 1:   *They had come for her in a wagon and taken her away to be buried. And then the cousins and aunts and uncles had come and tried to fill up the house. But they couldn't.*

Chapter 3:   *"Is my face clean?" he asked. "Can my face be too clean?" He looked alarmed.*

Chapter 4:   *The dogs loved Sarah first.*

Chapter 6:   *The cows watched, their eyes sad in their dinner plate faces.*

Chapter 7:   *Do not miss the hills. Do not miss the sea.*

Chapter 8:   *"Women don't wear overalls," said Caleb, running along behind her like one of Sarah's chickens.*

Chapter 8:   *"And then I can go to town. By myself." "Say no, Papa," Caleb whispered beside me.*

Chapter 9:   *Caleb burst into tears. "Seal was very worried!" he cried.*

Chapter 9:   *"Papa," he called. "Papa, come quickly! Sarah has brought the sea!"*

Journey

Chapter 1:   *What would pictures tell me? And the people? What would pictures tell me of my grandmother, so secretive; my grandfather, tall and blunt?*

Chapter 2:   *In the background a dog leaped into the air to grab a ball, his ears floating out as if uplifted and held there by the wind. But my mother looked silent and unhearing.*

Chapter 3:   *"I've got him for a whole hour while Mama weeds the garden," he said happily, untangling Emmett from the sling. "To shape or ruin his lima-bean brain. What shall it be?"*

Chapter 4:   *Actually, Grandfather calls it a "dialogue" we're having. I call it a fight.*

Chapter 5:   *I have spots in front of my eyes, Marcus! I can't read! Go away. Be a farmer.*

Chapter 6:   *Cat is a woman of action. She doesn't believe much in introspection.*

Chapter 8:   *But it was the family pictures that consumed him and drove us into hiding.*

Chapter 10:   *"It's good to eat with people who don't have food on their faces," said Cooper seriously. He paused. "But I love Emmett."*

Chapter 11:   *"A picture stops a little piece of time, good or bad, and saves it," he said.*

Chapter 12:   *…Grandma said that time was different depending on which journey you were taking—a trip to the mountains or a trip to get your tooth pulled.*

Conversations

Work in size-appropriate groups to write and perform the conversations that might have occurred in one of the following situations. If you prefer, you may use your own conversation idea for characters from *Sarah, Plain and Tall* or *Journey*.

Sarah, Plain and Tall

- Sarah and William talk about Sarah's leaving. *(2 people)*
- Sarah talks with the three aunts. *(4 people)*
- Sarah meets Hilly (the old housekeeper) on the train. *(2 people)*
- Matthew and Jacob discuss horses and farming. *(2 people)*
- Rose, Violet, Anna, and Caleb discuss stepmothers. *(4 people)*
- Sarah and Jacob discuss their future. *(2 people)*
- Sarah, Maggie, and Anna plan Sarah's wedding. *(3 people)*
- Caleb meets William on his boat. *(2 people)*
- Anna meets the three aunts. *(4 people)*
- William and his wife visit Jacob and Sarah on the farm. *(4 people)*
- Jacob and William compare fishing and farming. *(2 people)*
- Jacob, Sarah, Matthew, Maggie, and Anna discuss Caleb and Violet's upcoming wedding. *(5 people)*

Journey

- Liddie talks with her parents about leaving Cat and Journey with them. *(3 people)*
- Their papa comes to visit with Cat and Journey. *(3 people)*
- Liddie apologizes to Cat and Journey. *(3 people)*
- Cat and Journey talk with their mama and papa about the "old days." *(4 people)*
- Grandma talks about her upcoming concert with Cat and Journey. *(3 people)*
- Cat, Journey, Cooper, and Emmett share their future dreams. *(4 people)*
- Cooper and Cat plan their marriage and future. *(2 people)*
- Grandma, Liddie, and Cat plan Cat's wedding. *(3 people)*
- Journey and Emmett discuss grandfather and "Trot, Trot to Boston." *(2 people)*
- World famous photographer (Journey) discusses his journeys with Cat, Cooper, and Emmett. *(4 people)*
- Journey tells his little boy about his first driving experiences. *(2 people)*
- Cat tells her grandchildren about her work as a botanist. *(3 people)*

Bibliography

Fiction

Beatty, Patricia. ***Behave Yourself, Bethany Brant.*** (Morrow, 1986)

Brink, Carol Ryrie. ***Caddie Woodlawn.*** (Macmillan, 1973)

MacLachlan, Patricia. ***Arthur, for the Very First Time.*** (Harper & Row, 1980)

> ***Cassie Binegar.*** (Harper & Row, 1982)
>
> ***The Facts and Fictions of Minna Pratt.*** (Harper & Row, 1988)
>
> ***Mama One, Mama Two.*** (Harper & Row, 1982)
>
> ***Seven Kisses in a lRow.*** (Harper & Row, 1983)
>
> ***The Sick Day.*** (Pantheon, 1979)
>
> ***Through Grandpa's Eyes.*** (Harper & Row, 1980)
>
> ***Tomorrow's Wizard.*** (Harper & Row, 1982)
>
> ***Unclaimed Treasures.*** (Harper & Row, 1984)

Martin Jr., Bill and John Archambault. ***Knots on a Counting Rope.*** (H. Holt & Company, 1987)

Wilder, Laura Ingalls. ***By the Shores of Silver Lake.*** (Harper & Row, 1939)

> ***Farmer Boy.*** (Harper & Row, 1933)
>
> ***Little House in the Big Woods.*** (Harper & Row, 1932)
>
> ***Little House on the Prairie.*** (Harper & Row, 1935)
>
> ***Little Town on the Prairie.*** (Harper & Row, 1941)
>
> ***The Long Winter.*** (Harper & Row, 1940)
>
> ***On the Banks of Plum Creek.*** (Harper & Row, 1937)
>
> ***These Happy Golden Years.*** (Harper & Row, 1943)

References & Teacher Resources

Ferrell, Robert H. and Richard Natkiel. ***Atlas of American History.*** (Facts on File, 1991)

Hoy, Jim and Tom Isern. ***Plains Folk.*** (University of Oklahoma Press, 1987)

Owens-Knudson, Vick. ***Photography Basics.*** (Prentice-Hall, 1983)

> ***Pinhole Photograph.*** (University of Wisconsin OshLosh, 1991)

Schlissel, Lillian. ***Women's Diaries of the Westward Journey.*** (Schocken Books, 1987)

Stewart, Elinore Pruit. ***Letters of a Woman Homesteader.*** (Houghton Mifflin, 1982)

Trelease, Jim. ***The New Read-Aloud Handbook.*** (Penguin, 1989)

Cookbooks and Crafts

Carlson, Laurie. ***Kids Create!*** (Williamson Publishing, 1990)

Garson, Eugenia, ed. ***The Laura Ingalls Wilder Songbook.*** (Harper & Row, 1968)

Pierce, Charles, ed. ***The New Settlement Cookbook.*** (Simon & Schuster, 1991)

Walker, Barbara M. ***The Little House Cookbook.*** (Harper & Row, 1979)

Walker, Mark. ***Creative Costumes for Any Occasion.*** (Liberty Publishing Company, 1984)

Answer Key

Page 11

1. Accept appropriate responses.

2. Did Mama sing everyday? Did Papa sing, too? What did I look like when I was born?

3. There were many reasons why Jacob would advertise for a wife. Neighbors are far and few between. Town is a day's ride away, so it is hard to meet women. The children need a mother. Jacob is lonely. Their neighbor Matthew had written to ask for a wife and mother for his children, and everyone likes Maggie.

4. Caleb reads and reads the letters so many times that the ink begins to run and the folds tear. He keeps the letters with him, reading it in the barn, in the fields, by the cow pond—and always in bed at night.

5. Sarah tells them that she can sing.

6. Anna and Jacob do their chores: shoveling out the stalls and laying down new hay; feeding the sheep; sweeping and straightening and carrying wood and water. Then they wait and watch.

7. Sarah brings sea shells and sea stones.

8. When Sarah says "winter," he thinks it means Sarah will stay.

9. Anna thinks that with her hair pulled back, she would look a little like a daughter of Sarah's would look.

10. She cries, she shouts, and shakes her fist at the turkey buzzards; she won't let Caleb and Anna go near it; she stays out until Papa brings her back in the night by lantern; then she sits on the porch alone.

Page 16

1. Accept appropriate responses.

2. Accept appropriate responses.

3. They are neighbors of the Wittings who came to help Jacob plow a new field for corn. Maggie was a mail order bride from Tennessee. They brought Sarah some chickens and plants for a garden.

4. Sarah misses the sea, her brother, William, and the three old aunts.

5. There are always things to miss, no matter where you are.

6. Sarah wants to learn how to ride a horse and drive the wagon.

7. A tree blows over near the cow pond. The wild roses are scattered on the ground. One field is badly damaged and has to be replanted.

8. Caleb and Anna are afraid that Sarah will not come back.

9. The package contains three colored pencils—blue, gray, and green.

10. Answers will vary.

Page 21

1. Accept appropriate responses.

2. Cat gave him the camera in one of her fits of cleanliness.

3. Journey gets very upset. He starts defending his mother and making excuses for her. Then he cries.

4. Journey stares at his grandfather angrily. Journey does not understand why his grandfather is always taking photos of him, even while he is crying.

5. Her reply is, "No, it wasn't the camera, Journey. It was your mama. Your mama always wished to be somewhere else."

6. Cooper is a neighbor boy who is best friends with Journey and "besotted" with Cat. He babysits for his baby brother, Emmett.

7. The first picture is one of Grandfather playing with baby Emmett.

8. Grandfather's reply is, "A thing doesn't have to be perfect to be fine. That goes for a picture—for life. Things can be good enough."

9. His mama had torn the pictures up before she left.

10. Cat believes that Journey isn't sick, just hiding out.

Page 24

Labeled parts of a camera should look like this.

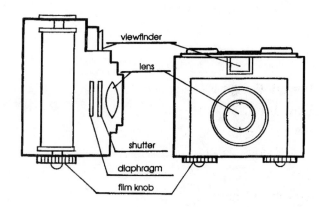

Answer Key *(cont.)*

Page 27

1. Accept appropriate responses.
2. Bloom is the cat that came and stayed.
3. Grandma is not fond of cats because they are always after her birds. But she secretly loves Bloom.
4. Bloom finds the pictures under the bed in Mama's room.
5. Journey wants to put all the pictures back together and make everything all right.
6. Journey and Cooper try patching all the pictures together. Cooper finally leaves after realizing that it is impossible. They see that Mama has even torn up pictures of Grandma. Then Journey realizes that Mama is never coming back.
7. Answers will vary.
8. Journey suddenly remembers the strange feeling he had when Mr. MacDougal gave him a kiss on his forehead. And because he wants to remember what it was like— he stands on tiptoe and kisses Grandfather.
9. Grandfather turns the tool room into what he calls his office, but it is actually a darkroom for developing pictures.
10. Journey discovers papa's face is a face that he does not remember. He also realizes that once his parents loved him.

Page 32

1. Answers will vary.
2. Answers will vary.
3. Caleb and Journey are searching for a mother.
4. Sarah experienced the death of a lamb. Journey discovered that his mama tore up all his baby pictures and those of the rest of the family. Accept other reasonable answers.
5. Sarah cries, shouts and shakes her fist at the turkey buzzards. She doesn't let Anna or Caleb near the lamb. Sarah stays out until night and Papa brings her back. She sits on the porch alone.
6. Journey stays in bed for two days as if he were sick.
7. Sarah and the Wittings slid down the haystack and swam in the cow pond.
8. Maggie reminds Sarah that "There are always things to miss—no matter where you are."
9. Grandfather tells Journey that "A thing doesn't have to be perfect to be fine—things can be good enough."
10. Sarah discovers that although she will always miss her old home, she would miss the Wittings more if she ever had to leave. Journey realizes that Grandfather, not his papa, was the one he remembered when he was a young child and that once his parents loved him.

Page 43

Matching: *Sarah, Plain and Tall*

1. c, 2. j, 3. g, 4. a, 5. h, 6. e, 7. f, 8. b, 9. i, 10. d

Matching: *Journey*

1. c, 2. f, 3. d, 4. i, 5. b, 6. h, 7. j, 8. g, 9. a, 10. e

True or False

1. false 2. true 3. true 4. false 5. true 6. false

Essay

Answers will vary. Accept all reasonable and well supported responses.

Page 44

Accept all reasonable and well supported responses and explanations.

Page 45

Perform the conversations in class. Ask students to respond to the conversations in several different ways, such as, "Are the conversations realistic?" or, "Are the words the characters say in keeping with their personalities?"